DeathWish
Therapy

By

Michael Lambert Jr.

Welcome to *DeathWish: Therapy*, a
visual journey through the depths
of the unseen—spirits, ghosts,
demons, and angels, each figure
crafted from the raw edges of my
imagination. In these pages, you'll
find sketches that have served as
companions in my own battles,
visual metaphors that captured the
darkness and the light within. This
book isn't just art; it's an offering
of vulnerability, a testament to the
therapeutic power of creation.
Thank you for stepping into this
space with me, where line and
shadow become expressions of
resilience and release.

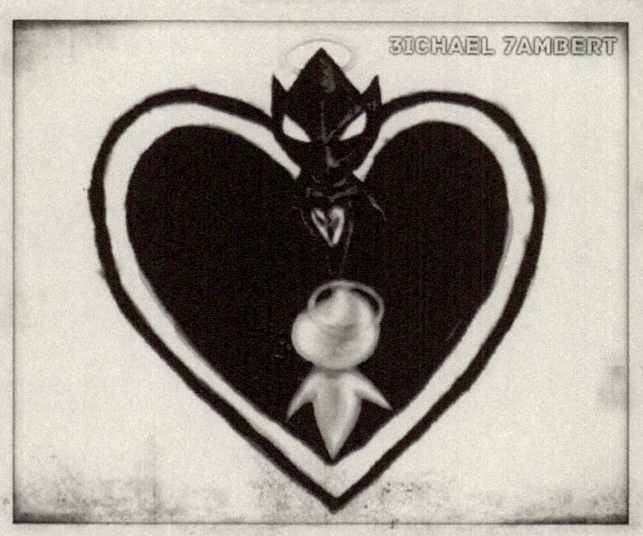

3ICHAEL 7AMBERT

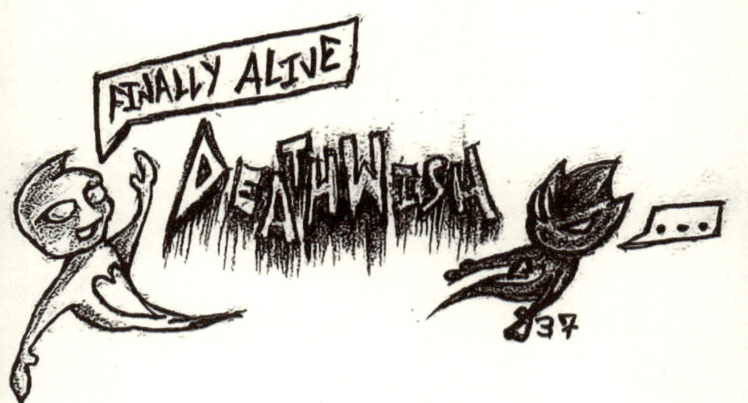

FINALLY ALIVE
DEATHWISH

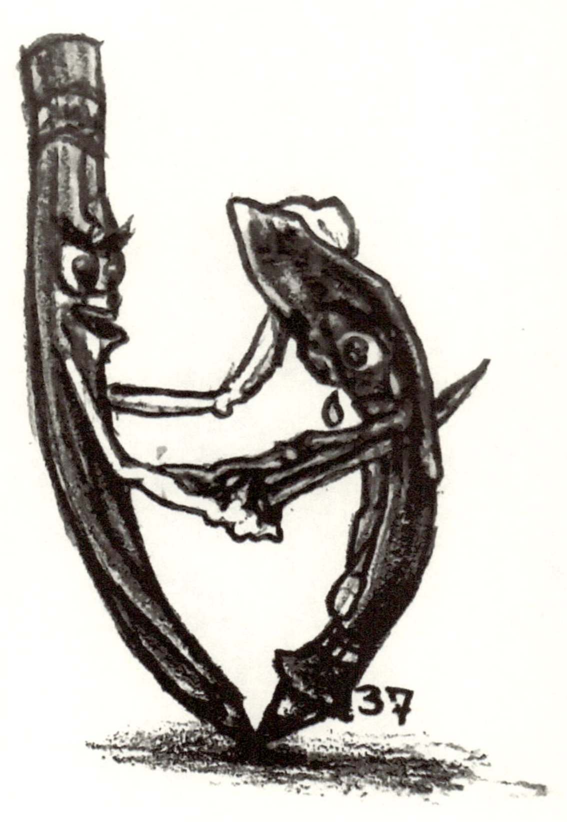
37

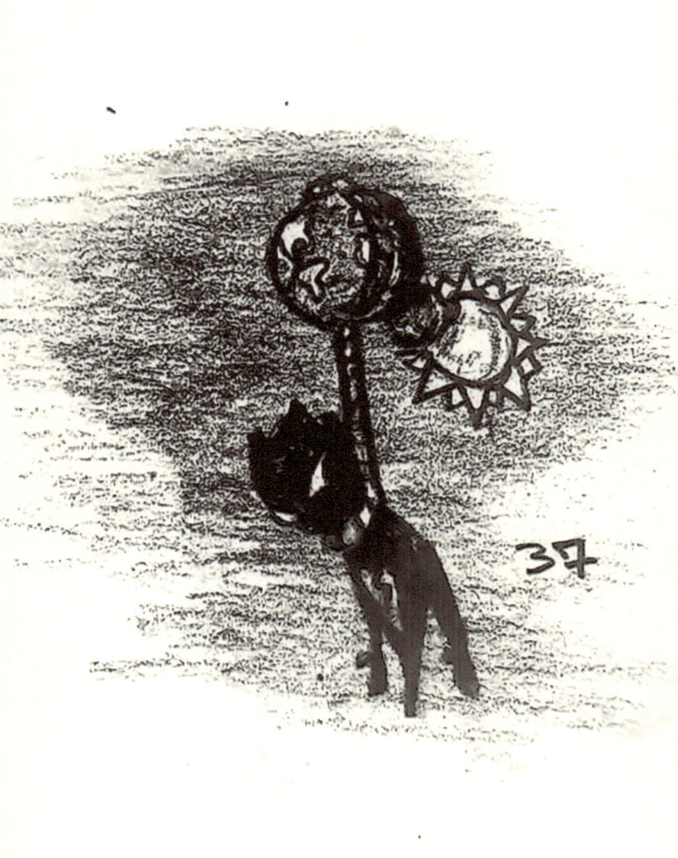

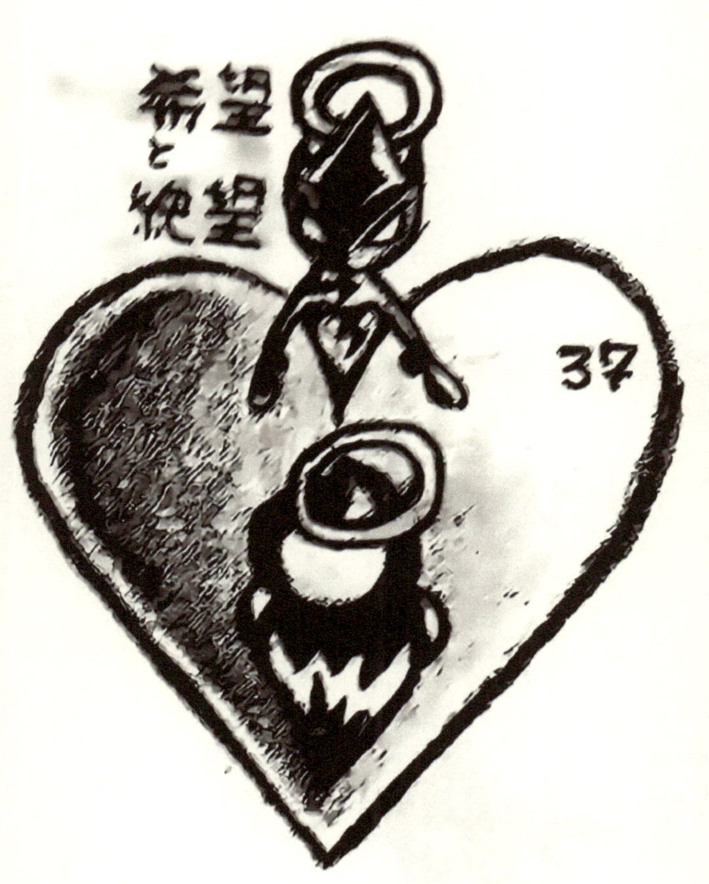
希望
と
絶望
37

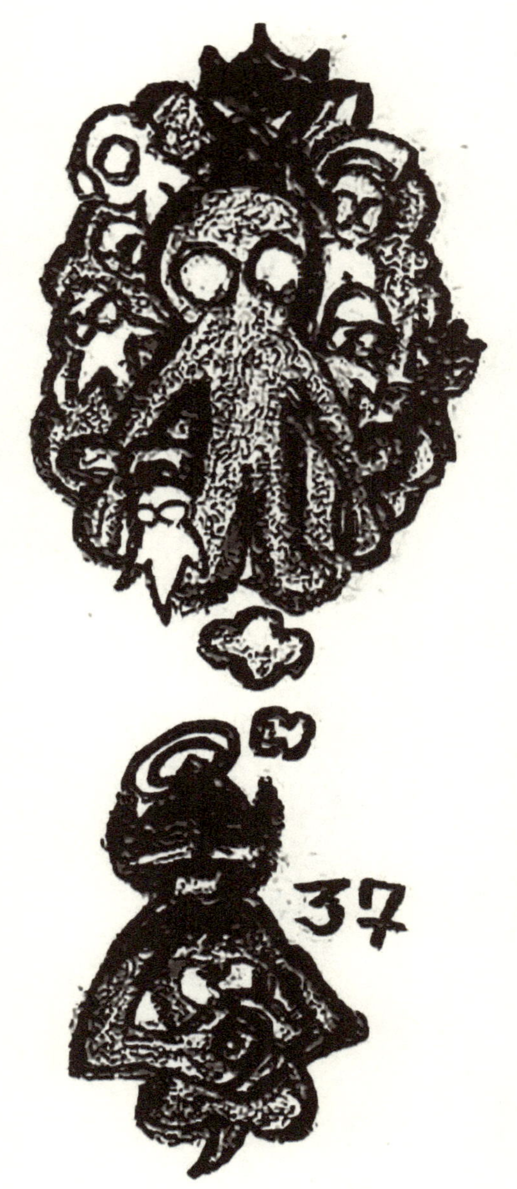

37

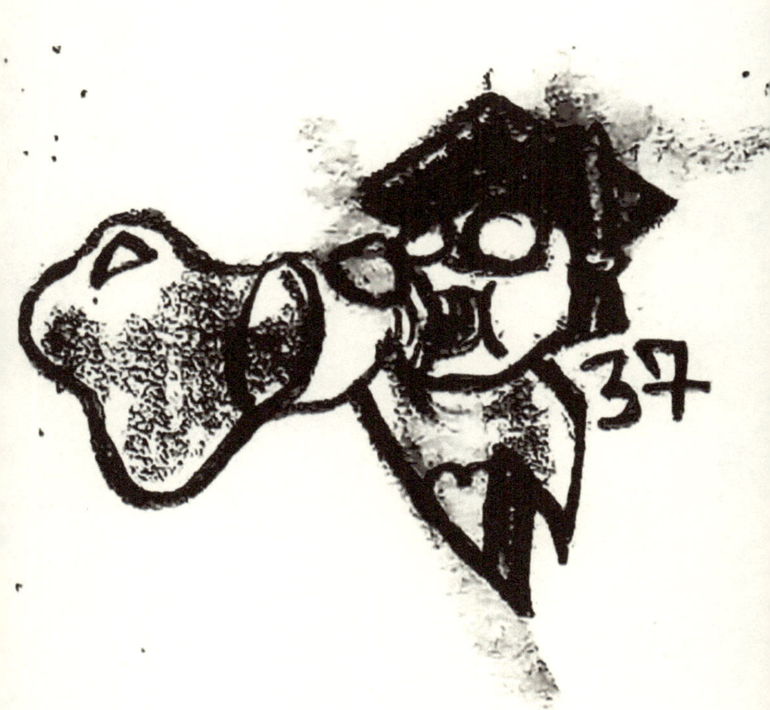
37

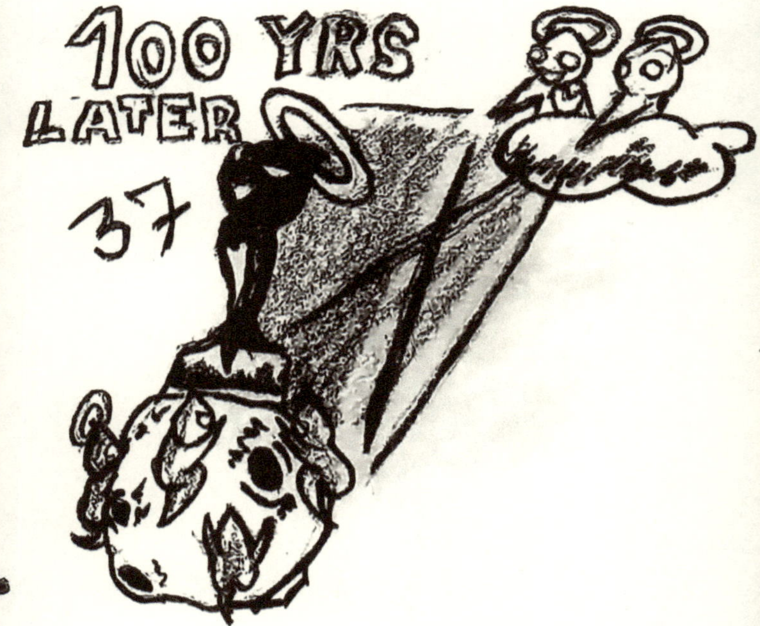

100 YRS
LATER
37

LOVE
YOU
BEST
BUDDY
37

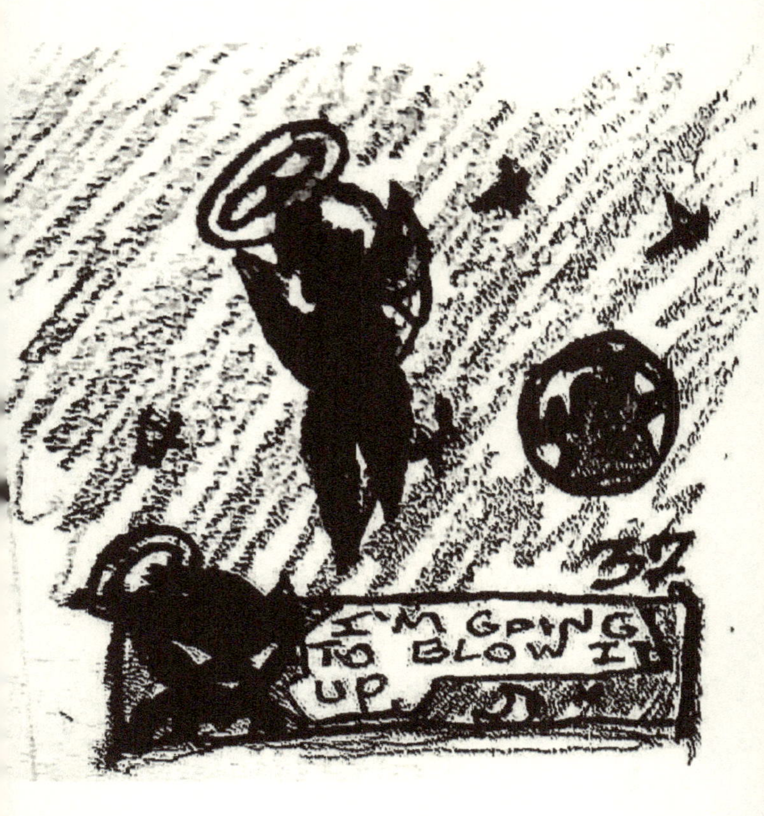

I'M GOING
TO BLOW IT
UP
37

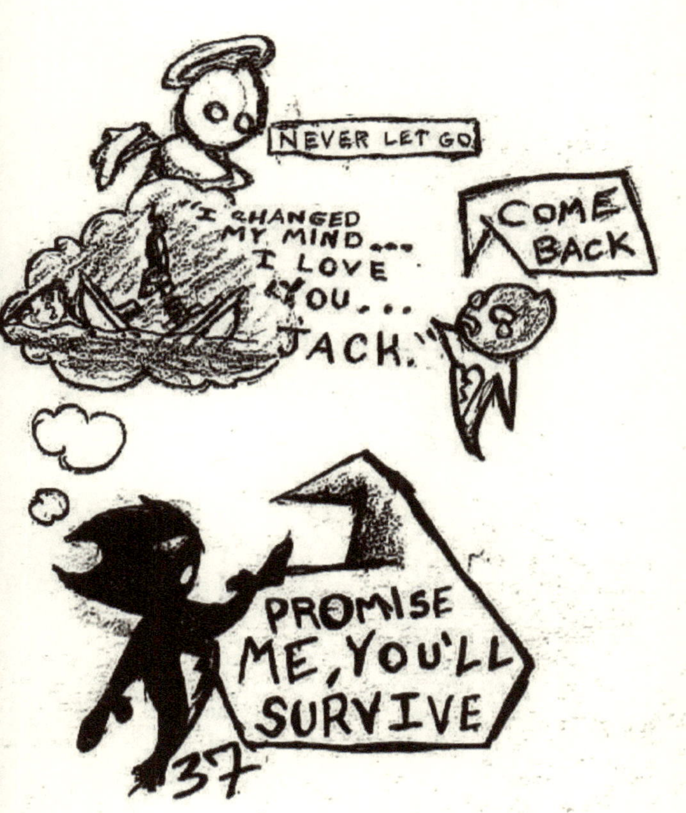

NEVER LET GO
I CHANGED MY MIND.... I LOVE YOU... JACK.
COME BACK
PROMISE ME, YOU'LL SURVIVE
37

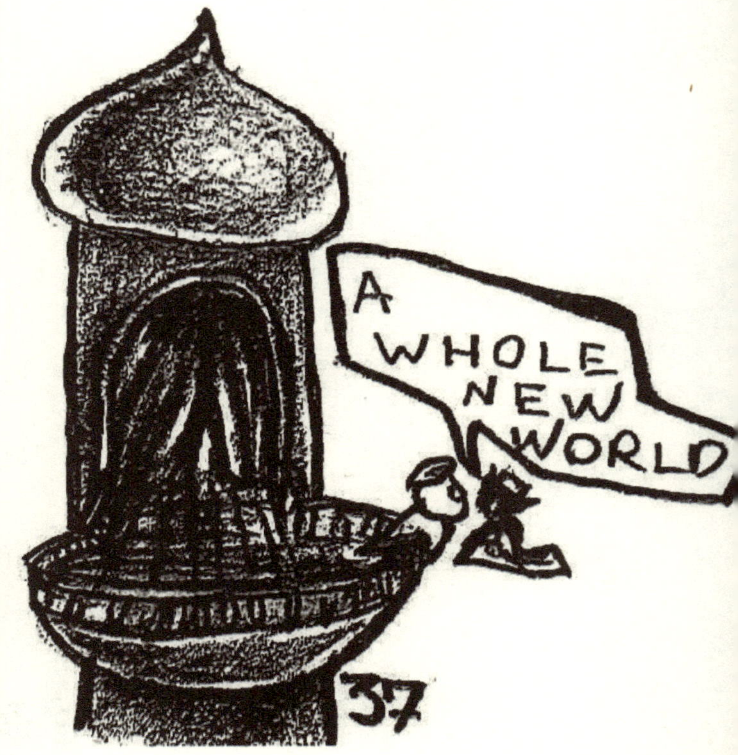
A
WHOLE
NEW
WORLD
37

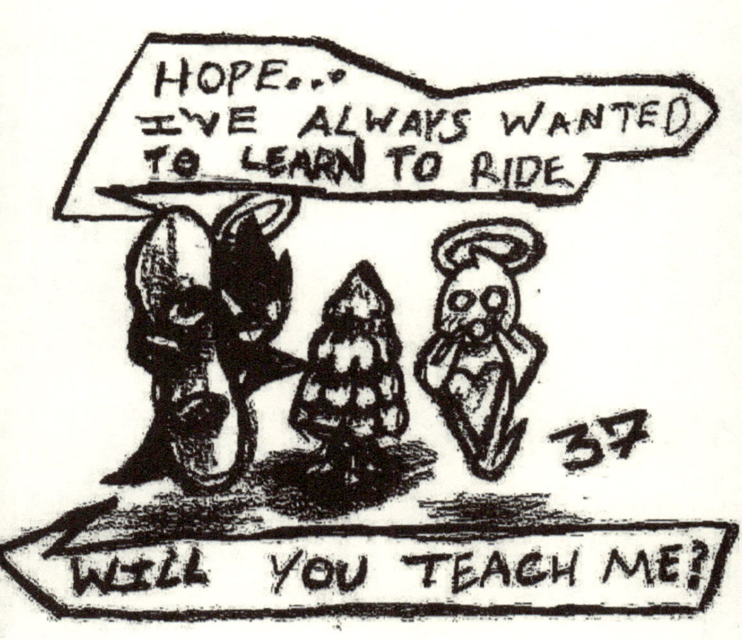

HOPE...
I'VE ALWAYS WANTED
TO LEARN TO RIDE
37
WILL YOU TEACH ME?

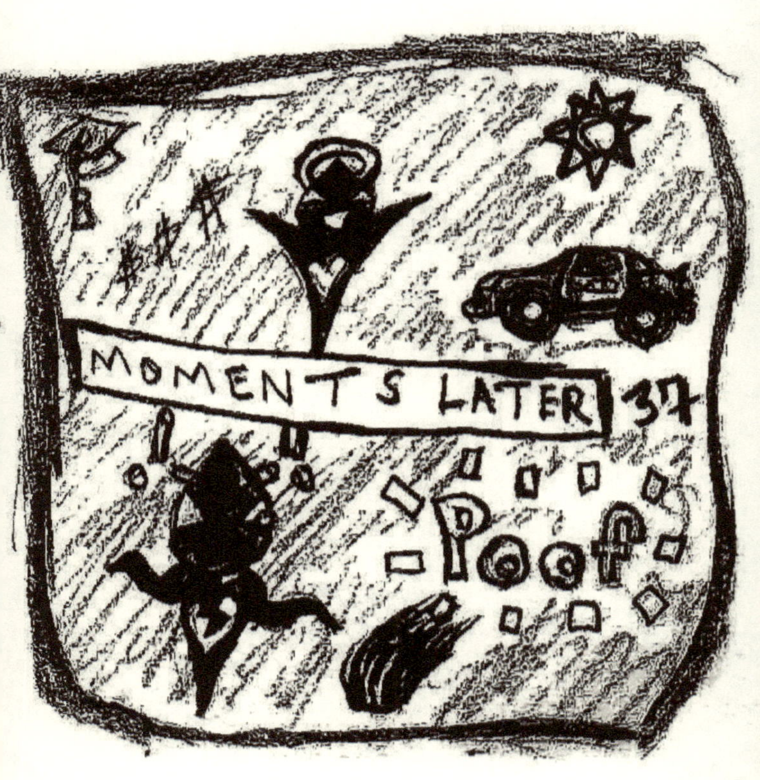

MOMENTS LATER
37
Poof

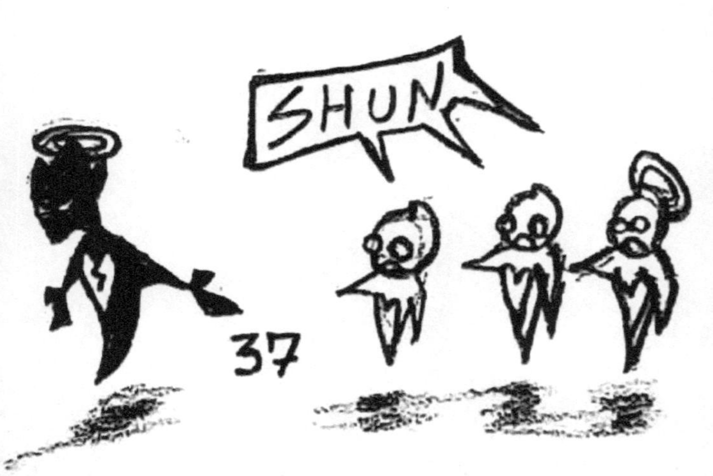

SHUN
37

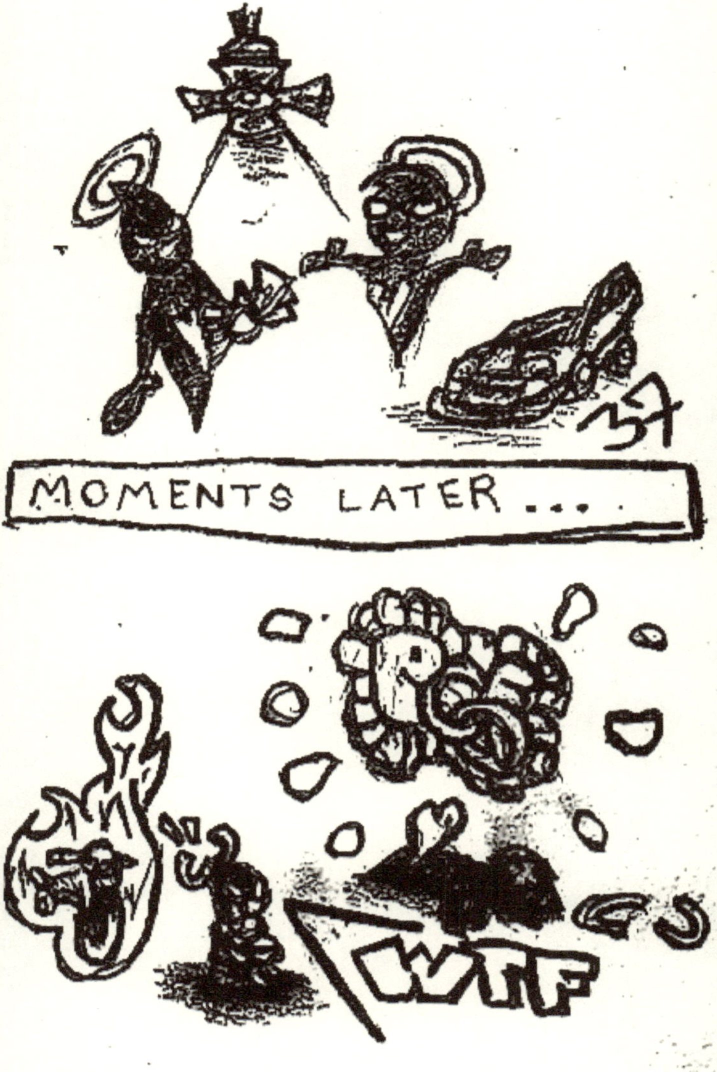

MOMENTS LATER ...
WTF

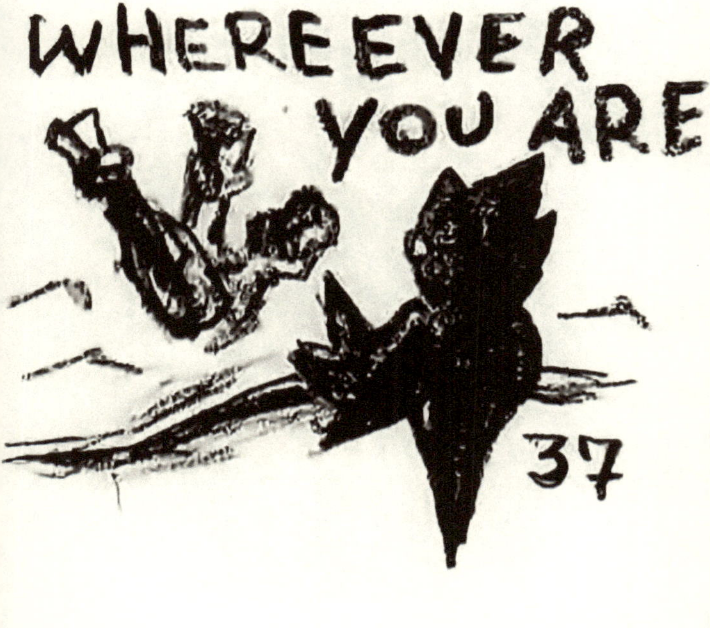

WHEREEVER
YOU ARE

37

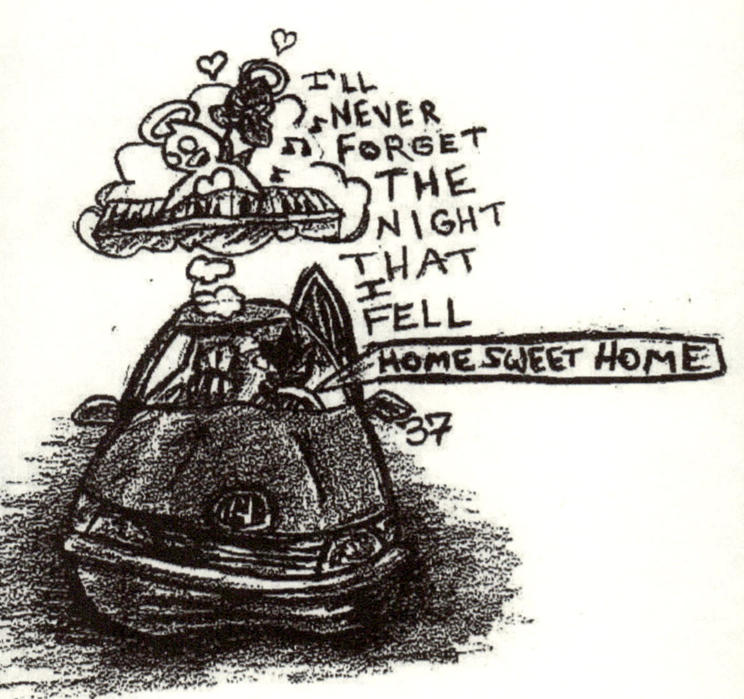

I'LL
NEVER
FORGET
THE
NIGHT
THAT
I
FELL
HOME SWEET HOME
37

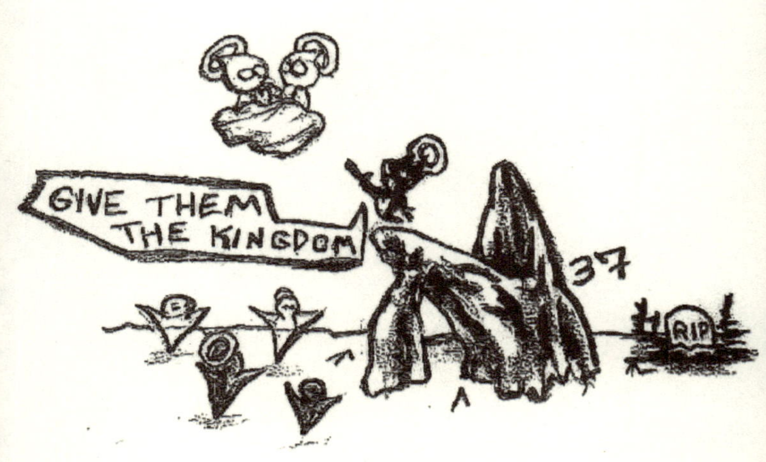

GIVE THEM
THE KINGDOM
37
RIP

MY NAME IS HOPE
37
DESPAIR

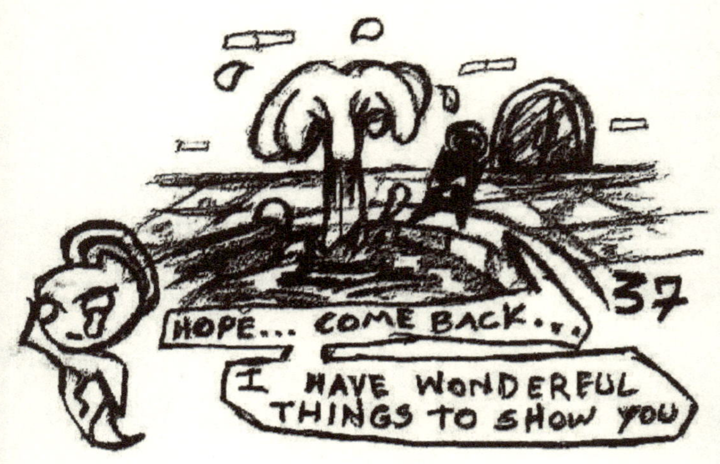
HOPE... COME BACK...
37
I HAVE WONDERFUL
THINGS TO SHOW YOU

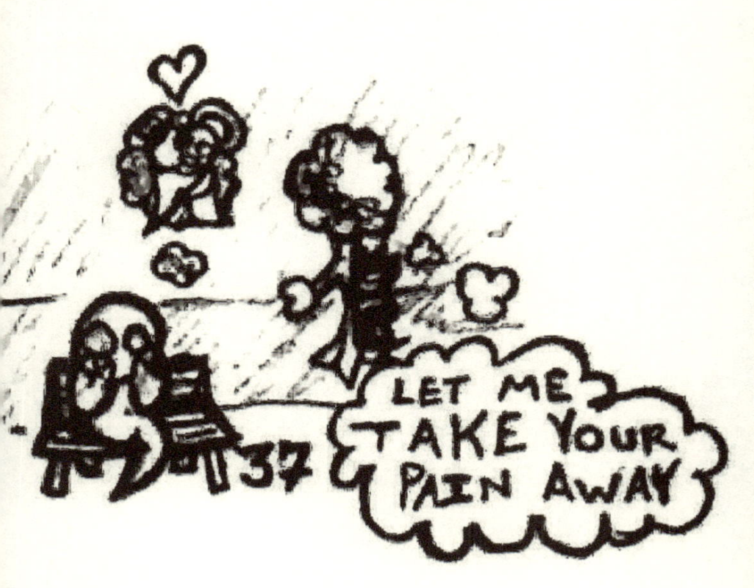

LET ME
TAKE YOUR
PAIN AWAY
37

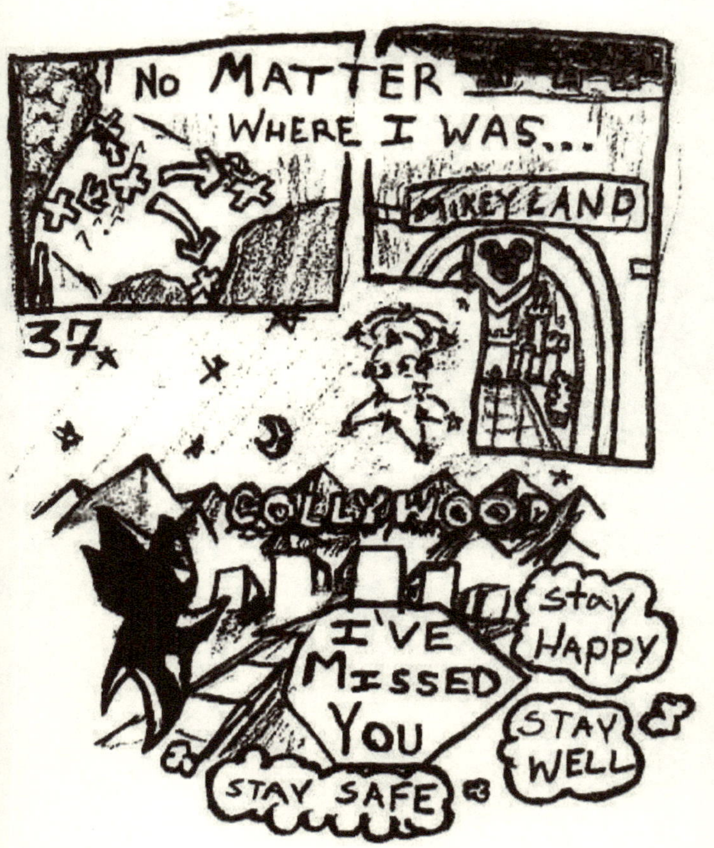

NO MATTER WHERE I WAS...
37
MIKEY LAND
COLLYWOOD
I'VE MISSED YOU
STAY HAPPY
STAY WELL
STAY SAFE

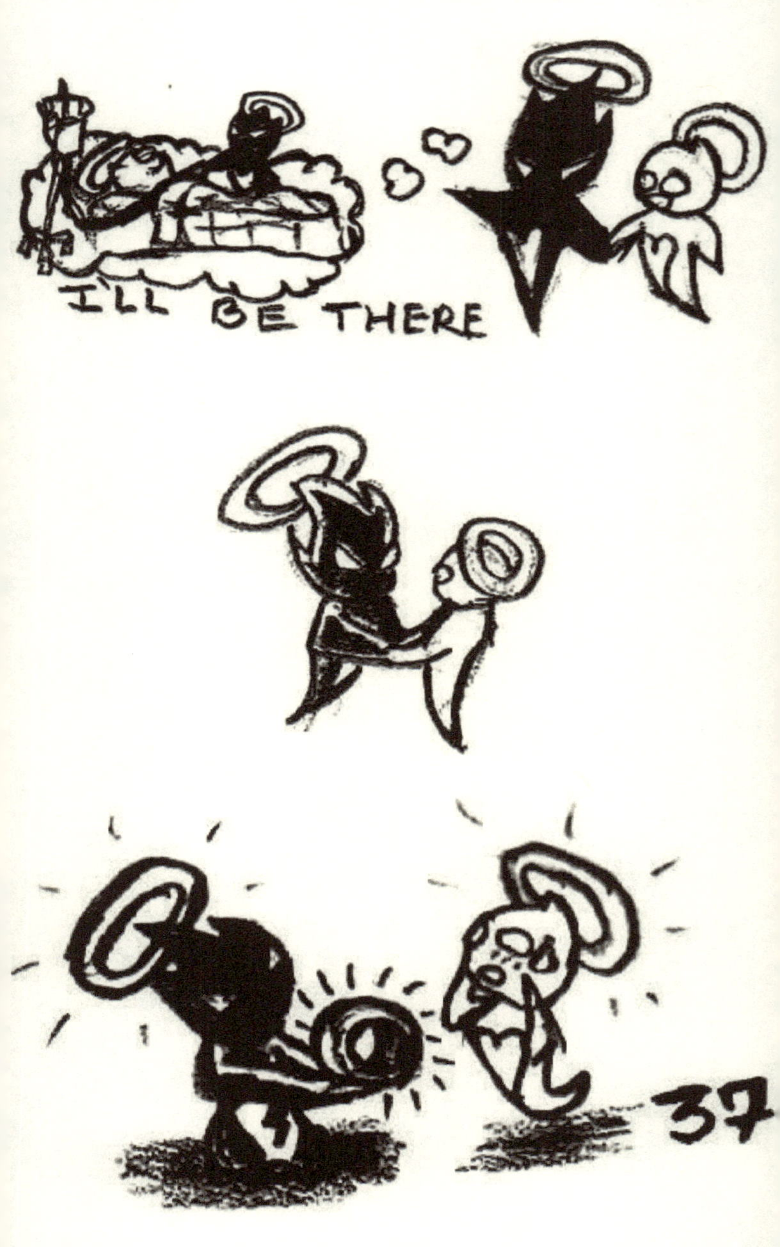

ILL BE THERE
37

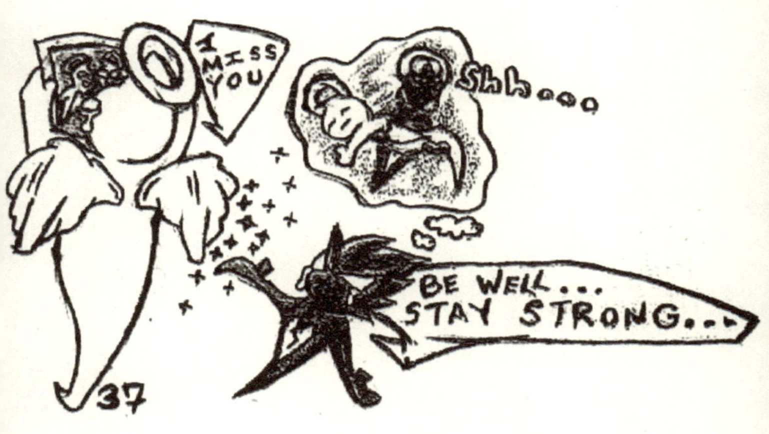
I MISS YOU
Shh...
BE WELL...
STAY STRONG...
37

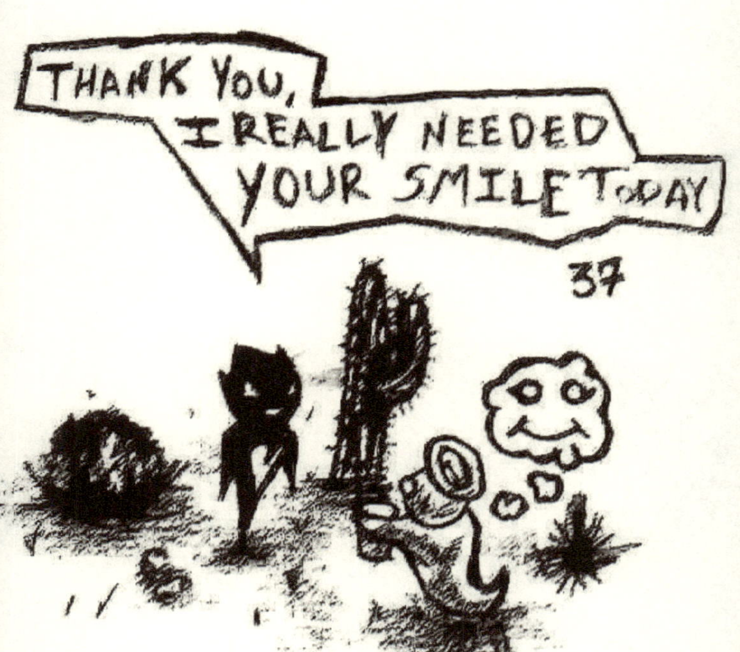
THANK YOU, I REALLY NEEDED YOUR SMILE TODAY
37

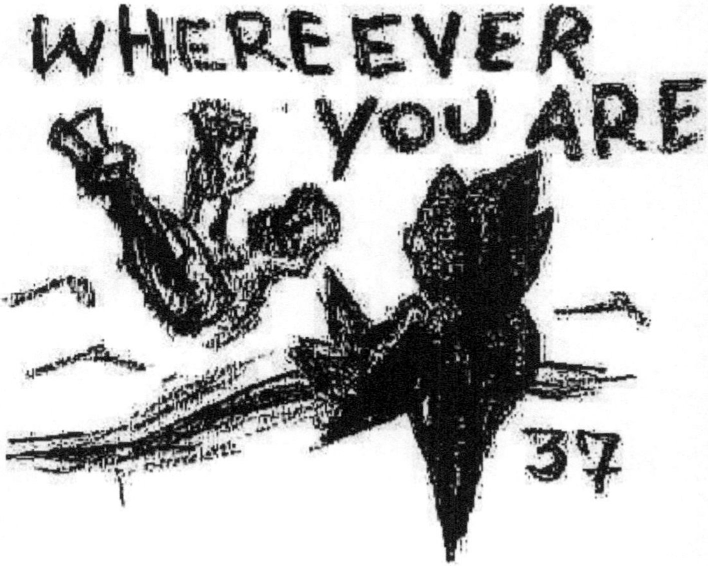

WHEREEVER
YOU ARE
37

40 YRS LATER

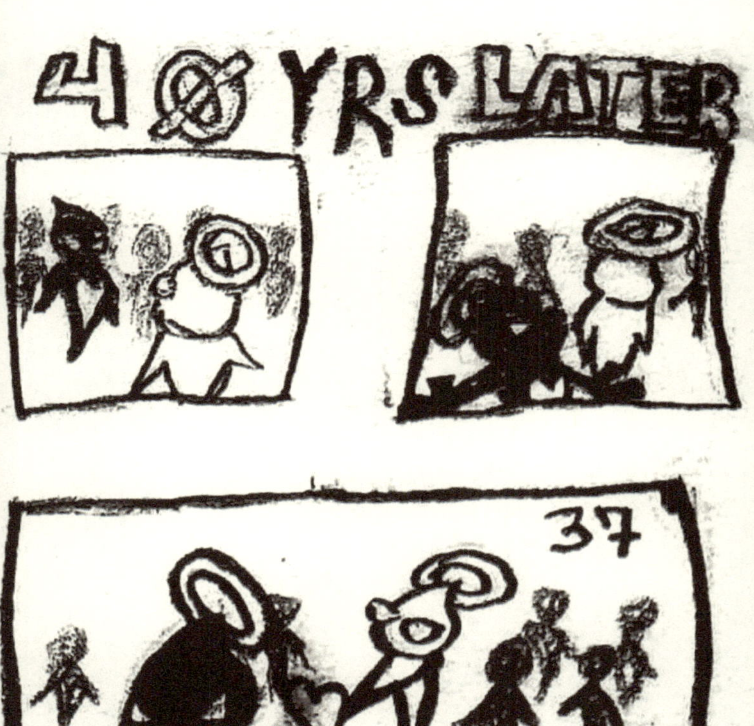

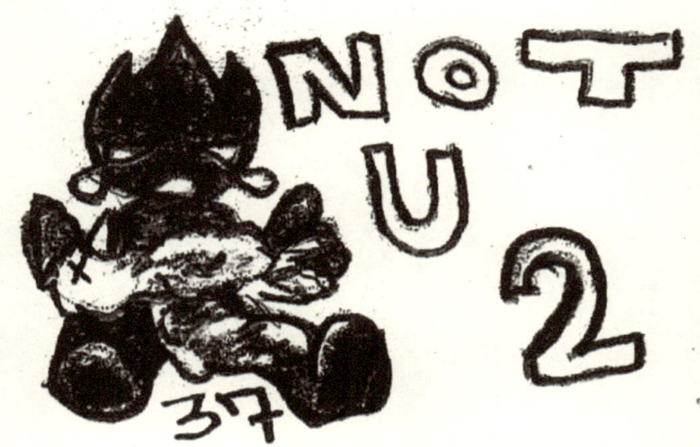
NOT
U
2
37

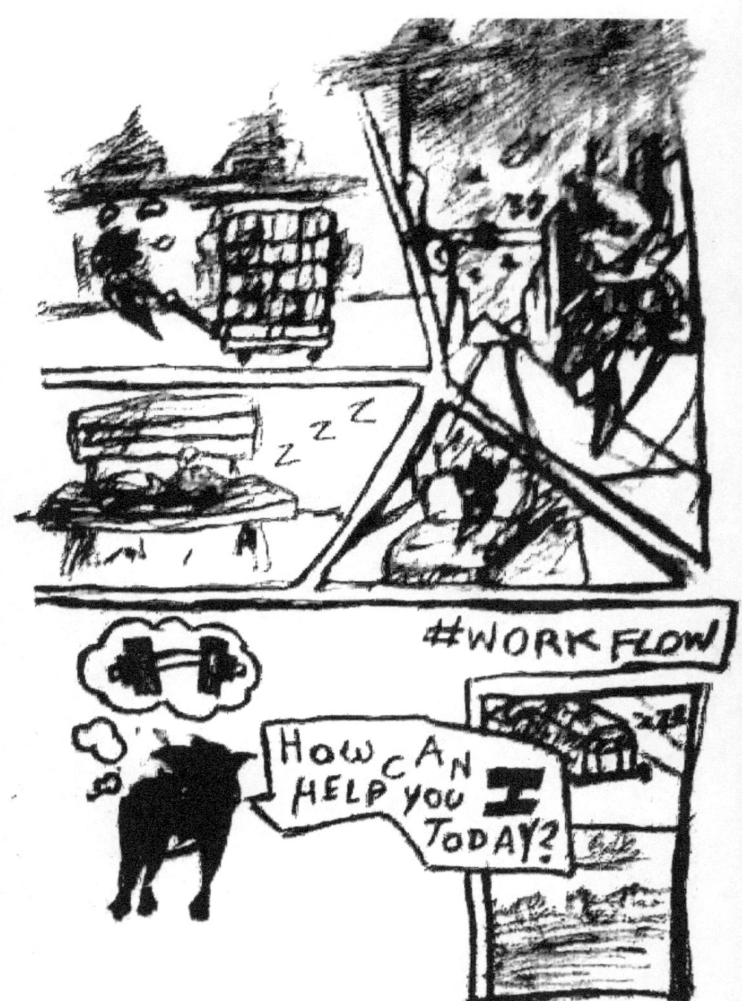

zzZ
#WORKFLOW
HOW CAN I HELP YOU TODAY?

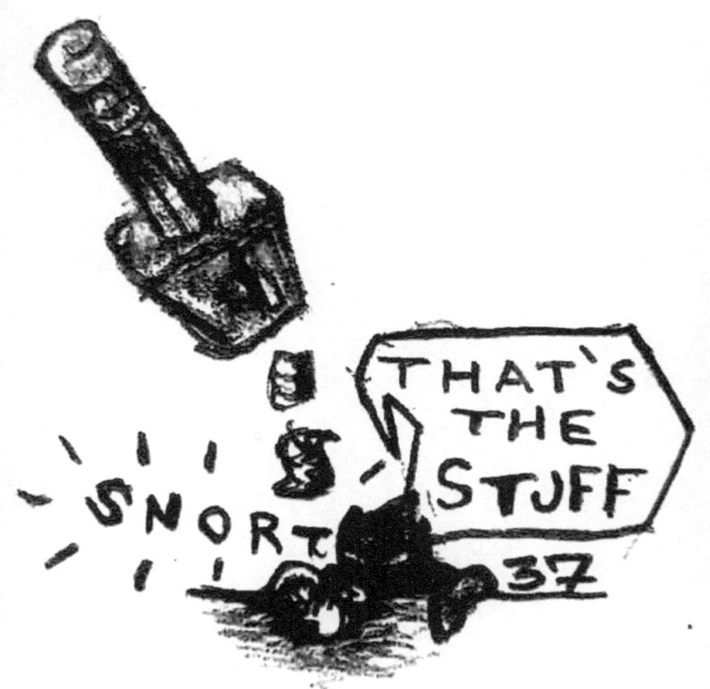

SNORT
THAT'S THE STUFF
37

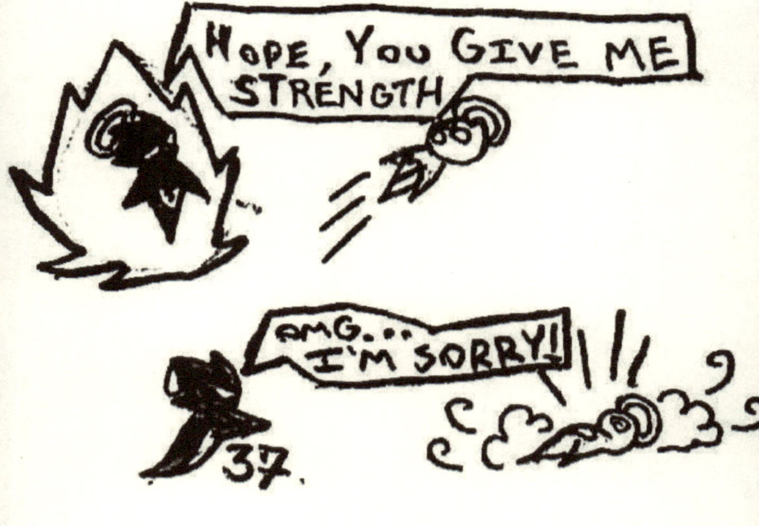

HOPE, YOU GIVE ME STRENGTH
OMG... I'M SORRY!
37.

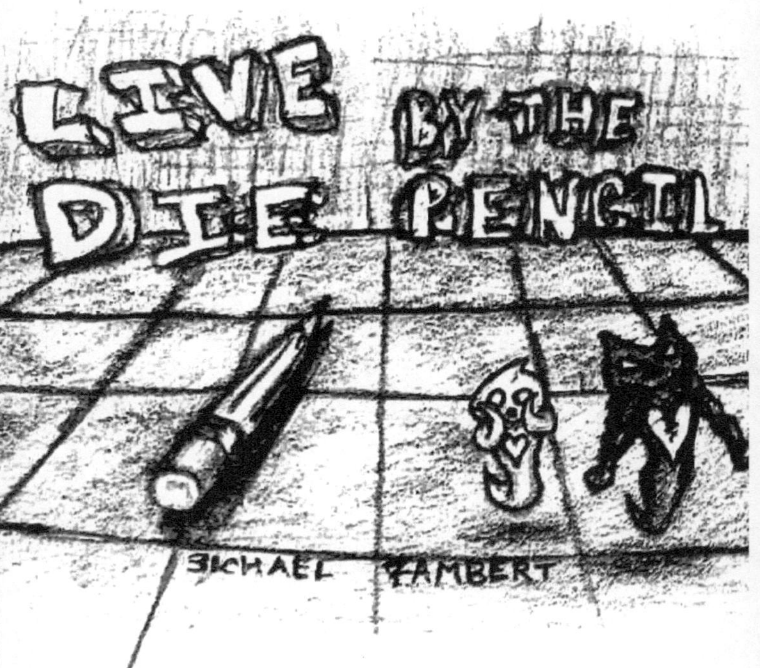

LIVE
BY THE
DIE
PENCIL
3ICHAEL YAMBERT

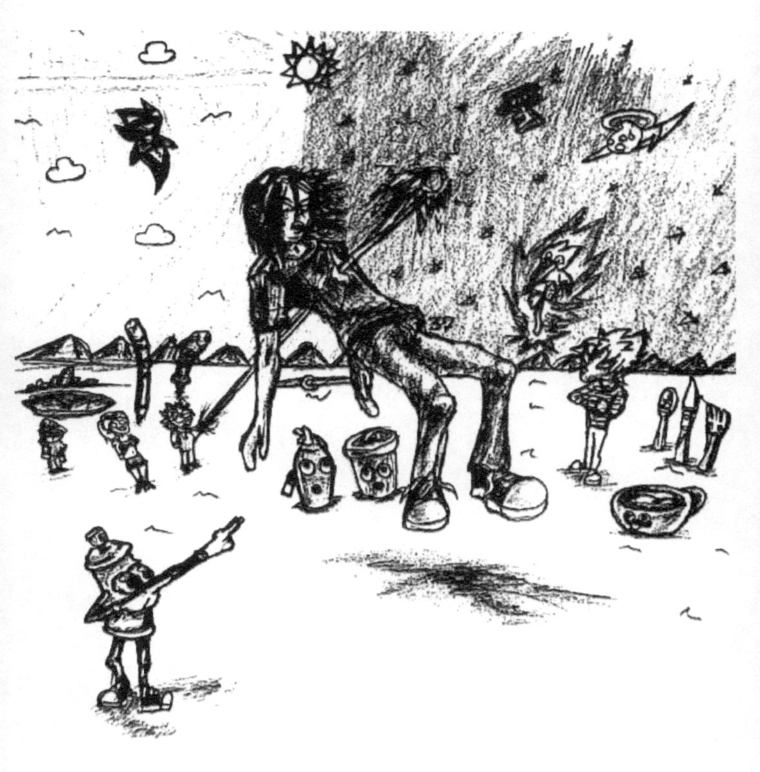

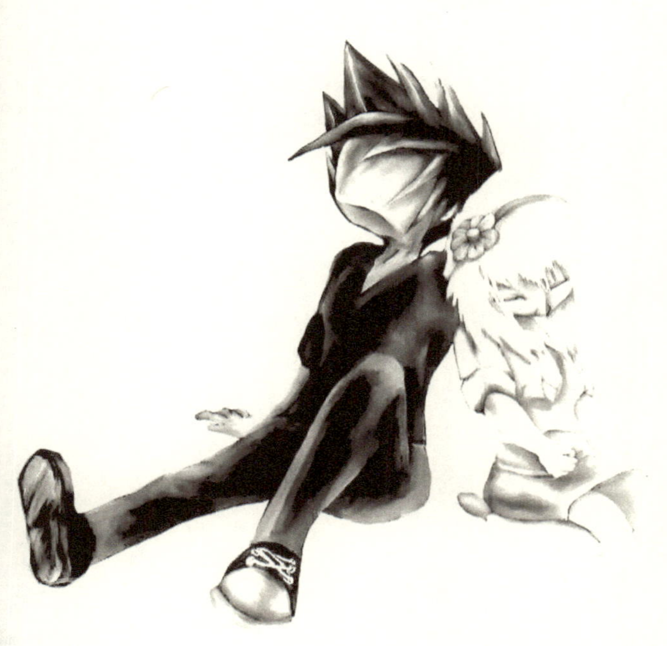

www.ingramcontent.com/pod-product-compliance
Lightning Source LLC
Chambersburg PA
CBHW031221160726
47992CB00006B/2848